Soviet Manipulation of "Religious Circles," 1975-1986

Emerson Vermaat

Soviet Manipulation of "Religious Circles,"

1975-1986

Aspekt Publishers

Soviet Manipulation of "Religious Circles," 1975-1986

© 2016 Uitgeverij ASPEKT
© Emerson Vermaat

Amersfoortsestraat 27, 3769 AD Soesterberg, Nederland
info@uitgeverijaspekt.nl - http://www.uitgeverijaspekt.nl

Cover: Maarten Bakker
Inside: Maarten Bakker

ISBN: 9789463380997
NUR: 680

All rights reserved. No reproduction copy or transmission of this publication may be made without written permission.

Introduction

The founders of communism, Karl Marx and Friedrich Engels, were well aware of the irreconcilability of religion and "dialectical materialism." "Religion," Marx wrote, "is the sigh of the oppressed creature, the heart of the heartless world... It is the opium of the people. To abolish religion as the illusory happiness of the people is to demand their real happiness."[1]

Vladimir Ilyich Lenin could not agree more. In 1917 he was the first to achieve power over a state in which Marxist doctrine was proclaimed the only legitimation of political power. Lenin's problem, however, was not whether to abolish religion but *how* to abolish it. He realized that at least in the short term some compromises were necessary. And his was not an easy task to face. The powerful Russian Orthodox Church (ROC) still had a grip on the profoundly religious Russian people. Lenin was aware of this, even in the years preceding the Bolshevik victory of 1917. "The Marxists," Lenin instructed his followers, "have to be consistent in their tactics in regard to religion."

They must agree that Marxism is materialism and, as such, "relentlessly hostile to religion." Therefore, "we must combat religion - that is the ABC of all materialism and consequently of Marxism." But, said Lenin, this is only part of the message. Marxism goes further and says: "We must know *how* to combat religion."[2]

Merely to impose atheism would simply do more harm than good; therefore, long-term strategy of the Marxists cannot be based on short-term tactics. It is essential that religion be used to pave the way for its own destruction. When religious groups or individuals play a "progressive role" and organize a strike, for example, Marxists should support them, and the atheist element in Marxism should be played down. In this, Lenin went further than the ultra left among his own followers. He even allowed priests into the party, provided they did not propagate their religious views within it:

> "The contradiction between the spirit and principles of our program and the religious convictions of the priest would in such circumstances be something that

concerned him [that priest] alone, his own private contradiction, and a political organization cannot put its members through an examination to see if there is no contradiction between their views and the Party program."[3]

These were Lenin's words eight years before the communists actually took power. It was, although in embryonic form, the same sort of "united front" concept that the Soviets would later apply so successfully. According to this concept, communists and noncommunists should cooperate to achieve certain common goals, but in the end only the communist side will prevail, destroying or absorbing the noncommunist elements.

After Lenin's death, the practice of allowing "progressive priests" into the party was soon abolished. After an initial period of friction between church and state, the Russian Orthodox Church gave in to the rulers. Although a "Decree on the Separation of Church and State" had been proclaimed in 1918, the new rulers continued the czarist tradition of using the church for their own political ends, to impress foreign, not domestic, audiences. Stalin and his successors demanded that the church support Soviet "peace initiatives." And in return for some domestic freedoms, however limited, the church appeared to be quite willing to become an instrument of Soviet manipulation and deception operations:

> "By playing an active role in the movement for peace since its inception, the Russian Orthodox Church has supported the peace-loving policy of the Soviet Union with every means in her power and her voice is heard through the medium of her representatives who speak out at various international and inter-church forums for peace and security."[4]

The Role of the Russian Orthodox Church in the World Council of Churches

One of the most conspicuous inter-church forums in which the Russian Orthodox church participates is the Geneva-based World Council of Churches (WCC). By 1961, the Soviet government no longer objected to Russian Orthodox membership in the WCC, which it had previously portrayed as an instrument of the cold war. Instead, the government showed a clear interest in politically manipulating the wider and still largely pro-Western ecumenical movement.

Before 1961, the WCC had been somewhat outspoken on matters of ideology and policy of communist party states. Thus, the WCC had clearly condemned the North Korean attack on its sovereign southern neighbour as an "act of aggression."[5] Representatives from churches in Eastern Europe were upset by this, and Dr. T. C. Chao of the People's Republic of China even resigned as one of the WCC presidents.

Metropolitan Nikodim and Patriarch Pimen in Moscow. Both were entirely devoted to the cause of the Soviet Union (USSR) and suppressed dissidents who opposed their pro-Soviet line.

After 1961, WCC criticisms of communist governments and policies were muted. It seemed as if, suddenly, WCC spokesmen and WCC meetings were careful not to offend the leadership of a church that had just joined the WCC community and that it was afraid to lose. The Russians, on their part, left the impression that they certainly would reconsider their membership in the WCC should it decide and unequivocally to condemn the human rights situation in Eastern Europe and the Soviet Union or to neglect major Soviet "peace initiatives."

An obvious example of this was the debate on religious freedom in the USSR at the Fifth

Assembly of the WCC in Nairobi, Kenya, in 1975. A letter from two Russian Orthodox dissidents, the priest Gleb Yakunin and the layman Lev Regelson, had come to the attention of the Assembly participants; it had, probably by mistake, been published in the Assembly's daily paper, *Target*. The letter bitterly complained about the WCC's failure to cope with the problem of religious freedom in the Soviet Union. "The believers of the Russian church never harbored any special illusions about the membership of the Moscow Patriarchate in the World Council of Churches; that act was sanctioned by the government during a period of extremely brutal persecution of religion and obviously followed the government's own strategic aims, quite remote from any consolidation of Christian positions in the modern world."

Pressured by the Russian Orthodox Church, the Assembly leadership initially sought to suppress the whole matter. But when the Assembly faced a draft text of a rather general statement on the ten principles of the recently signed Helsinki Final Act, Swiss delegate Jacques Rossel suddenly proposed that the statement should also express the WCC's concern about "restriction of religious freedom, particularly in the USSR."[6]

This proposal met with stiff resistance from the Russian Orthodox Church and its sister churches from Eastern Europe, who successfully managed to have a much more neutral and rather harmless final text adopted. This text merely pointed to the different situations in which churches in Western and Eastern European countries find themselves and did not explicitly refer to the persecution of religious believers in the Soviet Union.[7] Even this mild statement proved hard to swallow for the Soviets who, after the Assembly, bitterly complained about "the unfriendly spirit" at Nairobi.[8] With the help of the Hungarian member churches, the Soviets would tighten their grip on the WCC after Nairobi.

This example shows that if the facts concerning religious persecution could not be sufficiently concealed or suppressed, the state-controlled Russian Orthodox Church was even willing to resort to issuing threats, which could be construed as "blackmail." Another example of such blackmail also occurred at the Nairobi Assembly. During the debate on religious freedom, sentiment had grown against the candidacy of Metropolitan Nikodim - the head of the Russian Orthodox delegation - for the position of one of the WCC's

Metropolitan Nikodim (first person on the left) from the Russian Orthodox Church (ROC) was elected as one of the presidents of the World Council of Churches (WCC) in December 1975.

seven presidents.[9] At a certain stage, the prospects for this Russian hierarch, known for his loyalty to the Soviet cause, seemed rather glum. This suddenly changed after Third World church delegates were asked to attend a meeting of the Christian Peace Conference (CPC) in Nairobi, where they were reminded of the Russian church's influence with the Soviet government. Unfriendly behavior toward this church, consequently, could affect Soviet government's aid to the Third World governments and "liberation movements." Nikodim was subsequently elected as a WCC president. I heard this from Helene Posdeeff, a

Russian Orthodox lady from Munich who was present at this secret CPC meeting in Nairobi. She later wrote a chapter in a German reader on the Nairobi Assembly.[10]

From the perspective of the Soviet leadership, Russian Orthodox participation in the WCC proved very successful, particularly in foreign policy, peace, and disarmament issues. Although WCC rules and procedures do not provide for the right of veto, Russian Orthodox Church delegates participating in WCC meetings often managed to block or torpedo proposals or draft resolutions that were deemed hostile to the cause of Soviet policy. In this they were invariably assisted by delegates from Eastern-bloc-churches - particularly those active in the Prague-based Christian Peace Conference (CPC), considered to be a front organization controlled by the International Department of the Communist Party of the Soviet Union (ID-CPSU). They could, occasionally, also rely on some of their friends in the Third World whose ties to the CPC were well known.

This is not to say, however, that the Russian Orthodox Church and its allies actually controlled the WCC as a whole. There have also been examples

Dr. Lukas Vischer (third person from the left), a high ranking official from the World Council of Churches, listens to an address by Metropolitan Nikodim in Moscow. (Journal of the Moscow Patriarchate.)

of WCC statements that were unwelcome to the Russians but that they could not prevent. This was the case, for example, when the so-called officers of the WCC condemned the Soviet invasion of Czechoslovakia in 1968.[11] Occasionally, the Russian Orthodox Church was even forced into making inquiries after the fate of imprisoned clergy or other believers with the Soviet government at the request of the WCC.

On balance, however, the Russian Orthodox Church's grip on the WCC's decision making process seemed to be rather substantial. This particularly applied to the so-called "public issues," those that deal with international affairs and developments. The WCC's Commission on International Affairs (CCIA), for example, pursued a line usually quite favorable to the Soviets' foreign policy objectives. Very few of the CCIA's *Background Information* publications really contradicted Soviet viewpoints in the years between 1975 and 1986.

The CCIA also played an important role in the preparation of the WCC's Sixth Assembly in Vancouver, Canada, in 1983, because the WCC leadership was quite intent on preventing another human rights debate embarrassing to the Russian Church delegates. A few months before the Assembly, the WCC general secretary, Dr. Philip Potter, and the WCC Central Committee moderator, Archbishop Edward Scott, went to Moscow for talks with the Russian Orthodox hierarchy and officials of the State Council for Religious Affairs.[12] The latter body was the political instrument through which the Soviet government controlled the church and all other religious communities. It was attached to the Council of Ministers of the USSR and believed to be close to the Committee of State Security (KGB).

These careful preparations must have been responsible for the fact that a letter from Russian Orthodox clergyman Deacon Vladimir Rusak, complaining about measures against himself and other religious believers, was suppressed when the Vancouver Assembly met in the summer of 1983. Although addressed to all delegates of the Assembly, the letter was not even mentioned in any of the Assembly documents. The press was informed that "appeals from groups or individuals for World Council of Churches' intervention cannot be acted upon by the Assembly without the support of delegates of member churches, but will be followed up by the WCC General Secretary."[13] This meant, concretely, that the Russian Orthodox Church was asked to support the case of one of its own dissidents and to bring this case to the attention of the WCC before the WCC could really act on it. It is hard to imagine that the Russian Orthodox Church, which was controlled by the state, would ever do so out of its own accord. Not only was this church manipulated by the Soviet government but it also seemed to be well capable of manipulating such bodies as the World Council of Churches.

Other events at the Vancouver Assembly would provide sufficient examples of this. The most notable example was the Assembly's adoption of a long awaited "Resolution on Afghanistan."

Strangely enough, this resolution did not condemn the Soviet invasion of Afghanistan at all. On the contrary, a first condition, the resolution said, to "a comprehensive settlement" of the Afghanistan resolution would be "an end to the supply of arms to the opposition groups from outside."[14] It was as if those Afghans who defended themselves against a foreign invader were the aggressors, not the defenders. Had such an invasion not taken place in December 1979, however, there would be no armed resistance in Afghanistan. But now that the resistance movement opposed *Soviet* aggression, the WCC preferred to lay the blame on the defenders, and it did so because the Soviet government had a strong interest in a "realistic approach" to its own acts of armed intervention. The resolution also mentioned three other conditions to the "comprehensive settlement": "a favorable climate for the return of the refugees," "guarantees of the settlement by the USSR, the USA, the People's Republic of China and Pakistan," and, finally, "withdrawal of Soviet troops from Afghanistan in the context of an overall political settlement, including agreement between Afghanistan and the USSR."

Delegates from the Russian Orthodox Church described the resolution's text as "balanced and realistic" and left the delegates in the Assembly in no doubt that any other text would be unacceptable to them. They were supported by the CCIA and the Assembly leadership, who claimed that the draft text contained all the elements of similar UN proposals. Several attempts to have the text changed failed. Bishop David Preuss, a Lutheran from the United States, proposed, for example, that the first condition (to end the supply of arms to the resistance movements) be deleted and that the fourth condition regarding the withdrawal of Soviet troops be made the first. He further proposed to insert the word "immediate" before "withdrawal." All these suggestions were declined by the delegates of the Russian Orthodox Church; one of them even threatened that any such changes would "challenge our loyalty to the ecumenical movement."[15] Consequently, the Assembly approved the text as it stood.

One final point should be emphasized about the last condition to a "comprehensive settlement" mentioned in the resolution. This condition allowed Soviet troops to stay in Afghanistan until "an overall political settlement" involving Soviet participation could be reached. In other words, the invader was allowed to set the terms for his own withdrawal - a clear example of acquiescence to a form of power politics so often condemned by the WCC when the aggressor was not the Soviet Union.

The Russian Orthodox Church has also been very successful in pressing for the WCC's acceptance of Soviet positions on peace and disarmament. The findings of a WCC Hearing on Disarmament in 1981 and its subsequent endorsement by the WCC's Central Committee and Vancouver Assembly all fitted well with Soviet policy objectives and viewpoints. The eulogy of the peace movement, the strong condemnation of NATO's "double-track" decision of December 1979, and the call for a "nuclear freeze," "nuclear free zones," and "unilateral initiatives" were aimed at one side only. There was no specific condemnation of the Soviet military buildup that had preceded and provoked NATO's December 1979 decision to deploy modernized nuclear missiles. Any attempt to mention, for example, the Soviet SS-20 missiles in the Assembly's final documents was successfully resisted by the Russian Orthodox Church delegates.[16] Between Nairobi and Vancouver, Russian and East

European church delegates (particularly those from Hungary) strongly emphasized the implementation of a council "Program for Disarmament and Against Militarism and the Arms Race."

After the Vancouver Assembly, the Russian Orthodox Church - and consequently, the Soviet government controlling it - had every reason to be satisfied with the results. Addressing a meeting of the Soviet Committee for the Defense of Peace, Patriarch Pimen, head of the Russian Orthodox Church, pointed to the substantial contribution made by his and the other Russian member churches of the WCC to the deliberations at the Vancouver Assembly. He concluded that "the question of Christian peacemaking occupied a most important place."[17]

The Role of the Russian Orthodox Church in Manipulating "Religious Workers for Peace"

The Russian Orthodox Church has not confined itself to manipulating other Christian churches and bodies in the period under review; it laid special emphasis on mobilizing representatives and leaders of the world religions. That trends within the religious world were carefully monitored by the CPSU's International Department was no secret. As early as 1969, an International Conference of Communist and Workers' Parties in Moscow noted that "cooperation and joint action between communists and broad democratic masses of Catholics and adherents of other religions are developing in some countries."[18]

Four years later, a World Congress of Peace Forces was held in Moscow. During this event, the Russian Orthodox Church invited some 300 participants to a special meeting "to discuss the contributions of religions in the world towards the strengthening of international security and cooperation, towards strengthening of national would occasionally end up in far away parishes in Siberia or even in prison.[21]

Two years before his deportation from the Soviet Union, Alexandr Solzhenitsyn, himself an Orthodox believer, complained about this practice in his famous Lenten letter to Patriarch Pimen:

> "The entire administration of the Church, the appointment of priests and bishops, all of this is secretly managed by the Council for Religious Affairs. A Church dictatorially ruled by atheists is a sight not seen in two thousand years."[22]

While the Soviet government officially recognized separation between church and state, privately it required the church to operate as an extension of the politics of the state. This was what was really behind the church's attempts to mobilize the religious world "for peace." The first World Conference of Religious Workers for Lasting Peace and Just Relations Among Nations was held in 1977. Behind its lofty themes, such as "The Struggle for Peace - Common Cause of All Religions," representatives and observers from Muslim, Buddhist, and Christian religions including the WCC, the Holy independence and peace."[19] Here the groundwork was laid for future world conferences of religious leaders and workers that the Russian Orthodox Church was to convene after 1977. In order to prevent independent forces from having too much influence on the proceedings, all of these conferences were held in Moscow. Their participants were carefully selected, and in some cases Soviet embassies simply did not grant visas to uninvited journalists or critical observers.[20]

The real initiator of these events was not the church but the Soviet Politburo, which transmitted its orders through the State Council for Religious Affairs. This council was believed to be close to the KGB, which controlled a vast network of informants and agents throughout the church, including the Moscow Patriarchate, the Holy Synod, and the church's theological and educational institutions.

The church was forced to give substantial grants to the "Soviet Peace Fund," which financed peace propaganda at home and abroad and actively participated in the Soviet Committee for the Defense of Peace. Evidence indicated that bishops and clergy who refused to contribute to the cause of Soviet peace and propaganda would sooner or later find their ecclesiastical role diminished and

See, the Christian Peace Conference, the Lutheran World Federation, the Baptist World Alliance, the Conference of European Churches, and the All-African Conference of Churches did not resist the temptation to be used in a much larger Soviet peace offensive orchestrated by the International Department of the CPSU.[23]

Much wider publicity heralded the World Conference of Religious Workers to Save the Sacred Gift of Life from Nuclear Catastrophe held in Moscow in May 1982. The timing of this event was well chosen; in many of the West European countries and in the United States, powerful movements for nuclear disarmament were lobbying primarily against Western defense programs and NATO policies. This second Moscow conference for religious leaders was also better prepared than the previous one. In June 1981, representatives of different churches and religious associations in the Soviet Union were invited for consultation by Patriarch Pimen of the Russian Orthodox Church. Giving full support to the peace initiatives of the Soviet government, the meeting concluded that NATO and the United States were the root causes of a real threat of nuclear war. The meeting further called on "leaders and followers of all religions in the world to step up their efforts for disarmament and relaxation of tension."[24]

One month later, Patriarch Pimen made a widely publicized statement announcing a world peace conference of religious leaders. And in October 1981 an international preparatory meeting in Moscow, in which a representative of the World Council of Churches (WCC) also participated, appointed the Russian Orthodox Metropolitan Filaret of Minsk and Byelorussia as chairman of a "preparatory committee."[25]

As head of the influential department of External Relations of the Russian Orthodox Church (appointed in April 1981), Filaret played a key role in many of the peace initiatives of this church. His frequent visits to Western European countries between 1978 and 1983 were chiefly intended to encourage opposition movements to NATO. Filaret showed special interest in the Netherlands, where the peace movement had originated and was making a powerful impact in the late 1970s and early 1980s. Although the Dutch Russian Orthodox community was very small, Filaret and other Russian Orthodox dignitaries significantly stepped up their visiting program to the Netherlands, for reasons unknown. In October 1980 a Russian Orthodox Church delegation approached political parties and peace movements to discuss a number of Soviet initiatives. All these meetings bore no relation to religion whatsoever and were arranged by the third secretary for political affairs of the Soviet embassy, I. A. Krotov, who was suspected of being affiliated with the KGB.[26] Like one of his illustrious predecessors, Metropolitan Nikodim, Filaret was believed to be somewhat close to the KGB.[27]

Under the direction of Metropolitan Filaret, the preparatory committee and its steering group drew up the rules of procedure for the forthcoming world conference. These rules left very little room for dissenting opinion in the final documents, and plenary sessions were also heavily manipulated. When the World Conference of Religious Workers for Saving the Sacred Gift of Life from Nuclear Catastrophe actually took place in May 1982, independent-minded participants soon noticed, to their embarrassment, that there was very little room for serious debate. One representative of the Dutch peace movement, for example, was not given the floor after he had announced his wish to raise the issues of Soviet nuclear buildup and the Polish Solidarity movement.[28] Not refused the floor, however, was American evangelist Billy Graham, whose presence and prestige among conservative evangelicals the world over was used to upgrade the whole event in view of Western public opinion. Graham had been invited to the conference after he had established fruitful contacts with leaders in the Christian Peace Conference (CPC), which was considered to be a Soviet-front organization.[29]

As was the intention of the conveners, the final documents of the conference all reflected Soviet policy lines; subsequently, the documents received wide and favorable comments in the Soviet media.[30] From the perspective of Soviet policymakers, the conference had been a success. Nikolai Kovalski, an operative of the International Department of the CPSU in charge of penetrating and manipulating churches and religious circles, had no reason to complain:

> "People of goodwill, including believers and members of the religious community, are receiving a great spiritual and moral boost of Soviet foreign policy. It will be no exaggeration to say that in recent years major shifts have taken place in the

Russian Orthodox Metrolitan Filaret of Minsk (first person on the right) at a meeting of the World Council of Churches in Geneva (1984).

The World Council of Churches' Central Committee meeting in Geneva in 1984 where the Russians once again tried manipulate the debate on international issues.

religious community in matters of war and peace. It is no coincidence that the World Conference of Religious Workers for Saving the Sacred Gift of Life from Nuclear Catastrophe, the largest of its kind in recent years, was held in Moscow, the capital of the State which is staunchly defending the cause of peace."[31]

Not all major religious peace conferences were held in Moscow, however. In April of 1983, a Christian World Conference on Life and Peace was held in Uppsala, Sweden. Although the conference was an initiative of Nordic church leaders, the Russian Orthodox Church and the pro-Soviet Christian Peace Conference were well represented in the presidium and steering committee. Metropolitan Filaret of Minsk was one of the key speakers, and the final message of the conference appeared to be so consistent with the Soviet line that Soviet embassies were instructed to publish its text in full.[32] Moreover, the Uppsala conference received less negative publicity in the West than the Moscow-run events.

An important instrument of Soviet propaganda was the Soviet Committee for the Defense of

Peace. The Soviet Committee for the Defense of Peace was an integral part of the vast propaganda apparatus of the USSR and was believed to be close to the KGB. The Soviet Peace Committee played a dominant role in the WPC, the most important of all Soviet front organizations.

By 1983, with the proclamation of the International Year of Peace by the United Nations, the committee clearly saw the need to coordinate the UN's and others' initiatives to mobilize the religious world for more Soviet-inspired peace offensives. This, presumably, was the reason why the Soviet Committee for the Defense of Peace set up its own Public Commission for Contacts with Religious Circles for Peace in December 1983. With Metropolitan Filaret of Minsk as chairman, the stated purpose of the new commission, not surprisingly, was "to promote more effective ties between the Soviet champions of peace and foreign anti-war religious circles."[33]

The Role of Soviet Front Organizations

The Russian Orthodox Church was not the only instrument propagating Soviet policy lines within religious circles. Efforts to court religious circles were much broader and involved the full weight of the propaganda apparatus of the CPSU's International Department, which controlled some fourteen international front organizations.[34] Of these fronts, at least three have been instrumental in manipulating the religious world: the World Peace Council (WPC) in Helsinki, the Christian Peace Conference (CPC) in Prague, and the Asian Buddhist Conference for Peace (ABCP) in Ulan Bator, Mongolia.

Although religious figures have played a role within the WPC since its inception in 1949, it really began to focus attention on religious groups after its World Parliament of the Peoples for Peace in Sofia, Bulgaria, in 1980. Under the heading "Religious Circles for Peace," the WPC's program of action called for, inter alia, "meetings with leaders of various religions to offer the World Peace Council's cooperation and support in all initiatives taken by them for peace."[35] So far, the WPC had not been very effective in this respect. As a former Soviet front and propaganda forum, the WPC has been widely discredited, and by far most of those who participated in it were fellow travelers if not communists.

The WPC was heavily involved in the preparation of the Moscow World Conference of Religious Leaders in 1982. Contacts with church leaders and inter-church organizations such as the World Council of Churches (WCC) intensified. At the WPC's Peace Assemblies in Prague (1983) and Copenhagen (1986), religious participants held their own working sessions. In all these efforts, the WPC delegated much of the work to the Christian Peace Conference (CPC), a front organization created in 1958 to influence the ecumenical movement and churches in the West. In later years the CPC, creating regional organizations in Asia and Africa, was to broaden its scope to the Third World.

The only occasion when the Soviets really lost control over the CPC leadership emerged in

1968, when the CPC's Czechoslovak president, Joseph L. Hromádka, protested the Soviet invasion of his own country. In the preceding decade, Hromádka had shown himself to be quite loyal to the Soviet cause, even to the extent of defending the crushing of the Hungarian Revolution by Soviet troops in 1956. Soon after 1968, Hromádka was forced to resign and was succeeded by Metropolitan Nikodim of the Russian Orthodox Church - a political hardliner who also played a major role in the WCC's Executive Committee.[36]

The subsequent CPC leadership - President Bishop Dr. Karoly Toth of Hungary, General Secretary Lubomir Mirejovskiy of Czechoslovakia and Chairman of the Continuation Committee Metropolitan Filaret of Kiev - guaranteed the CPC's pro-Soviet direction. Although Bishop Toth was Hungarian, he was known for his absolute loyalty to Moscow; he seemed to be more committed to the cause of Marxism than to the cause of the church.[37]

The Russian Orthodox Church exerted tight control over the CPC through Metropolitan Sergey Fomin and Dr. Aleksei Buyevsky, both from the Moscow Patriarchate's External Relations Department. In early 1980, Fomin made a trip to the Netherlands to convince Dutch peace activists that the Soviet invasion of Afghanistan had been provoked by NATO's "double track" decision (modernization of intermediate-range nuclear missiles) of December 1979. Buyevsky was one of the most outspoken defenders of Soviet policy in numerous WCC meetings (as a member of the WCC's Central Committee) and numerous other international religious forums. Within the WCC, Buyevsky has had a hand in the drafting of many WCC documents on international affairs. I wrote already in 1977 that Buyevsky was possibly a KGB agent and this observation turned out to be a correct.

The Asian Buddhist Conference for Peace (ABCP), based in Ulan Bator, Mongolia, was founded in 1969 to mobilize the Buddhist world against the American military presence in Indochina and Asia. The ABCP propagated the Soviet line on all aspects of Soviet foreign policy, particularly with respect to Asian countries. It's Seventh General Conference in February 1986 in Vientiane, Laos, received a message from Soviet prime minister Nikolai Ryzhkov, wishing the conference every success and pointing out that "the Soviet government highly values the

"Peace Assembly" of the World Peace Council in Prague in 1983. I was there myself.

Demonstration in the Netherlands against NATO's Double-Track Decision. The Soviets and their East German alies tried to win over as many peace activists as possible.

activities of religious organizations in the name of peace and disarmament." Ryzhkov presented the Soviet Union as "a major Asian state" that therefore "gives priority attention to ensuring Asian security."

> "We highly appreciate the constructive peace initiatives of other Asian countries and fully support the idea of turning the Indian Ocean into a peace zone, proclaiming the Southern Pacific a nuclear-free zone, and setting up such a zone in Southeast Asia."[38]

These, presumably, would be the ABCP's marching orders for the years to come.

The ABCP was fully integrated in the Soviet front system. It's newly elected general secretary, Gelegjamtsyn Lubsantseren, had previously been employed by the World Federation of Democratic Youth (WFDY) in Budapest. *Buddhists for Peace,* the ABCP's official journal, paid much attention to the activities of the World Peace Council, the Christian Peace Conference, and other Soviet fronts.

The World Council of Churches and Soviet Fronts

Much more than was officially admitted by WCC staff members, Soviet fronts, particularly the WPC and the CPC, did play a role in manipulating this major ecumenical body. A special target was, of course, the WCC's Commission of the Churches on International Affairs (CCIA). Founded shortly after the war, the CCIA and its first director, O. Frederick Nolde, soon gained respect for their contribution to international legal documents on human rights and religious freedom. When the WCC was caught up with the radical movements of the 1960s, however, the need for a change was felt. Soon after the Uppsala Assembly of 1968, the old CCIA guard, basically Western in orientation, was replaced, and Dr. Leopoldo J. Niilus became the new CCIA director. Niilus's background was interesting: born in Tallinn, Estonia, in 1930, Niilus left for Argentina in 1948, where he graduated in law at the national university of Buenos Aires. He became an Argentine citizen and, as a Lutheran, soon became active in church circles. He also

Visit of a high level Russian Orthodox Church delegation to "Pax Christi Internationalis" in Vienna in November 1974. Sitting behind the table from left to right: Archimandrite Kirill, representative of the ROC at the WCC in Geneva and the contemporary patriarch, Metropolitan Nikodim and Bernard Cardinal Alfrink. Standing behind them and second person from the left (wearing glasses): Aleksei Buyevsky.
(Journal of the Moscow Patriarchate.)

showed interest in the work of the Christian Peace Conference in Prague. In 1968 he attended the CPC's Peace Assembly in Prague. This may be the reason why the Metropolitan Nikodim endorsed the appointment of an Estonian emigré as new CCIA director when such responsibility was that of the Executive Committee of the WCC.[39] With Niilus and his new staff, the CCIA soon took a decisively "left" turn.

Metropolitan Nikpodim (in front in the center) visits the WCC's Central Committee meeting in Utrecht, the Netherlands in August 1972. (Journal of the Moscow Patriarchate.)

Niilus's successor in 1981, Ninan K. Koshy from India, also had an interesting background. He served as a member of the CPC's International Secretariat in 1974. Both Niilus and Koshy were careful not to identify themselves too openly with known Soviet fronts, but they did not avoid staying in touch with them. In 1980 Niilus attended, as a WCC observer, the World Parliament of the Peoples for Peace sponsored by the World Peace Council and held in Sofia. And Koshy attended, also as a WCC observer, the next major WPC event in Prague in 1983.

I was there myself, covering that conference as a journalist.[40]

Both WCC (CCIA) and WPC took a leading position in the Special Committee on Disarmament of the nongovernment organizations affiliated with the United Nations. In 1982, WCC General Secretary Dr. Philip Potter and WPC President Romesh Chandra, a pro-Soviet communist from India, were among the officers of a conference on world public opinion and disarmament, convened by the special committee. The organizing secretary of the whole event, Victor W. Hsu, was also executive secretary of the CCIA and Potter served as the conference's president. Moreover all of the conference's three commissions were dominated by representatives of known Soviet fronts.[41]

Two years later, in March 1984, Romesh Chandra accepted an invitation by CCIA Director Ninan Koshy to participate in an "informal exchange of views" on the prevention of nuclear war, East-West relations, and similar issues. By that time, WPC plans for an International Conference on Nicaragua and for Peace in Central America were well under way. Together with a number of other Soviet fronts, such as the International Association of Democratie Lawyers (IADL) and the World Federation of Trade Unions (WFTU), the WCC's CCIA joined a preparatory committee - thus affiliating itself officially with an event initiated and largely sponsored by the WPC.[42] Mario Soares, the Portuguese prime minister at that time, successfully prevented Willy Brandt and other representatives of the Socialist International from attending this conference by informing them of its Soviet origins and inspiration.[43] (I myself met Willy Brandt in Nicaragua, but this was on another occasion and it had nothing to do with the WPC or the WCC.) On the one hand, however, it cannot be claimed that the WCC was *controlled by* the World Peace Council for, unlike the WPC, the WCC was not a Soviet front. On the other hand, it cannot be denied that Soviet instruments and fronts have successfully *manipulated* the WCC.

The role of the Christian Peace Conference in the WCC was more substantial. Subsequent CPC presidents all took part in major WCC conferences, shaping the outcome of the debate on international issues. In 1975, CPC President Metropolitan Nikodim of Leningrad was elected as one of the seven WCC presidents at the Fifth WCC Assembly in Nairobi. The CPC's influence

Ninan Koshy (in the center), director of the WCC's "Commission of the Churches on International Affairs" (CCIA), together with Romesh Chandra (on the left), the President of the pro-Soviet World Peace Council (WPC). Both were from India. Koshy died in March 2015, Chandra died in July 2016. (Journal of the Moscow Patriarchate.)

on the WCC was further exerted through Third World theologians and clergymen close to the CPC, such as Richard Andriamanjato of Madagascar, Julio de Santa Ana of Uruguay, and Metropolitan Paulos Mar Gregorios of India.

Before he became a member (and later a director) of the WCC's Commission on the Churches' Participation in Development (CCPD) in 1973, Julio de Santa Ana was a member of the International Secretariat of the CPC. He became one of the WCC's main promoters of "liberation theology." Metropolitan Gregorios, of the Syrian Orthodox Church of India, must be considered the most influential CPC theologian within the WCC. He attended the CPC's first major All-Christian Peace Assembly in 1961 and has been active in the CPC since. One year later, Paul Verghese (his actual name before he became Metropolitan Gregorios) became an associate general secretary of the WCC, and in 1983 the Vancouver Assembly elected him as one of the seven WCC presidents. By that time Gregorios could also claim the position of vice president of the CPC. In this capacity he often represented the CPC at other Soviet-controlled events. In 1983, for example, Gregorios addressed the Sixth General Conference of the ABCP.[44]

The year 1983 was rather busy for the Indian church leader, who also had to preside over (and partially prepare) an International Round Table Conference on Economic and Moral Implications of Nuclear Freeze that took place in Moscow. This event had been prepared by the Working Presidium of the 1982 World Conference of Religious Workers for Saving the Sacred Gift of Life from Nuclear Catastrophe, whose chairman

Conference in Moscow on "New Dangers to the Sacred Gift of Life" (February 1985). From left to right: Metropolitan Filaret of Minsk, Metropolitan Paulos Mar Gregorios from India (Moderator), the Rev. Dr. Richard Andriamanjato from Madagascar. (Journal of the Moscow Patriarchate.)

was Metropolitan Filaret of Minsk.[45] A primary aim of the Moscow Round Table Conference was to endorse recent Soviet proposals on nuclear freeze. The WCC showed its interest in the event by sending one of its CCIA executive secretaries, Dr. Erich Weingartner.

Gregorios would also be the moderator of similar round table conferences of religious workers and experts (all in Moscow, of course) in 1984 ("Space Without Weapons"), 1985 ("New dangers to the Sacred Gift of Life: Our Tasks") and 1986 ("Hunger, Poverty and the Arms Race").[46] In addition, Gregorios was also a high-level member of the World Peace Council.

Thus, his credentials as an international front figure seemed to be well established.

Gregorios's already significant role in the WCC further increased when the Vancouver Assembly elected him as one of the seven WCC presidents in 1983.

With Nikodim, who had died suddenly in 1978, no longer in the WCC's presidium, the Soviets needed a politically reliable successor. Using all available means - the Russian Orthodox Church, the Christian Peace Conference, and other channels - the Soviets therefore lobbied for Gregorios. Since he was a Third World candidate, this proved not too difficult.

As a WCC president, Gregorios used his position to influence WCC statements on international affairs - a field which had always had his special interest. In 1985 he was part of a small WCC delegation to Central America that expressed views solely in line with Cuban and Soviet policy. When in Nicaragua, the delegation conveniently refused to recognize representatives of peaceful opposition groups and the independent human rights commission, as well as the hierarchy of the Roman Catholic Church (RCC), and the WCC delegation confined itself to expressing solidarity with the Sandinista government and those supporting liberation theology. It was also Gregorios who, a few weeks later, reported on the delegation's visit to the WCC's Central Committee meeting in Buenos Aires.[47]

Metropolitan Paulos Mar Gregorios ("Paul Verghese") from the Malankarese Orthodox Syrian Church in India, played a very important role both in the World Council of Churches and pro-Soviet front organizations.

The Soviet Appraisal of Liberation Theology

Having its origins in Latin America in the late 1960s, liberation theology profoundly affected churches and theological institutions in other parts of the Third World and even in the West. As a Third World theology, it also became the dominant trend within the WCC. The Vatican in Rome was very critical, though.

In 1968 the Conference of Latin American Bishops (CELAM) meeting in Medellín, Colombia, produced a significant document on poverty and exploitation that is generally regarded as the signal for liberation theologians to develop a theology of liberation of their own. Although the bishops meeting in Medellín recognized that revolutionary insurrection could be legitimate in the case of "evident and prolonged tyranny,"[48] the more radical theologians and clergy went much further. They incorporated Marxist analysis into their theological framework.

Shortly after Medellín, the Peruvian theologian Gustavo Gutiérrez published his *Teología de la liberación.* Gutiérrez espoused a socialist order, that is, "social ownership of the means of production."[49] Gutiérrez and other liberation theologians also incorporated the concept of class struggle and the non-Marxist concept of "utopia" (meaning a denunciation of the existing order) in their theology.[50] They gave biblical concepts such as "exodus," "justice," "love," "salvation," and "Kingdom of God" an entirely political meaning. Some radical priests, like Camilo Torres in Colombia, joined communist guerrillas. Others became government ministers in Nicaragua after the Sandinistas - whose ideology was a strange blend of Marxism, Castroism, and religion - had assumed power in the summer of 1979. But today, liberation theology is no longer restricted to the Roman Catholic community. A whole range of Protestant theologians have developed their own liberation theologies, making an additional impact on Protestant theology as a whole.

It did not take long for Moscow to take note of these trends and developments. As early as 1969, an International Conference of Communist and Workers' Parties in Moscow noted:

> "The Catholic Church and some other religious organizations are experiencing an ideological crisis that is shaking their age-old concepts and existing structures. Cooperation and joint action between Communists and broad democratic masses of Catholics and adherents of other religions are developing in some countries... Communists are convinced that in this way - through broad contacts and joint actions - the masses of religious believers can become an active force in the anti-imperialist struggle and for profound social transformations."[51]

More explicit in its support for liberation theology and the rebellious priests in Latin America was a 1977 article in the Moscow journal *International Affairs*. Referring to "progressive currents in the Catholic Church which are trying to use some postulates of the Christian religion as a justification for radical social changes," the author, K. Khachaturov, praised "the strengthening of anti-imperialist trends in religious circles in Latin America."[52]

Eight years later, the Soviet weekly *New Times* carried an article in defense of Leonardo Boff from Brazil, one of the most influential liberation theologians. The article seized on the occasion when in 1984 the Vatican had reprimanded Boff for his deviation from Church doctrine. Calling Boff's opponents in the Vatican "the latter-day inquisitors," the article claimed that the liberation theology "recognizes the justice of the struggle waged by the rebel priests against dictatorial regimes and U.S. imperialism."[53] While liberation theology is not a Marxist theory, it nevertheless uses Marxist methods of analysis of the socioeconomic problems of society:

> "The theology of liberation challenged the basic thesis of the social doctrine of Catholicism, which propounds the universal conciliation of classes and renunciation of struggle for the social emancipation of the oppressed."[54]

Thus, Soviet Marxists did not recognize the ideological convergence between liberation theology and Marxist theory. In their more theoretical writings, they criticized liberation theologians for seeking to reconcile Christian faith and Marxism and reviving the non-Marxist concept of utopia. According to Marxist-Leninist doctrine, Utopian dreams cannot be part of the scientific analysis of Marxism.[55] But these differences on the theoretical level did not preclude practical cooperation or "unity of action."

It is significant that one of the most positive evaluations of liberation theology appeared in the *World Marxist Review - the* theoretical organ of the Soviet-oriented Communist parties run by the International Department of the CPSU. It described the development of liberation theology; links its opponents to the Pentagon, the CIA, and the Vatican; and finally concluded that this theology "provides fresh evidence that atheists and believers, Marxists and Catholics can and must act in a united front against imperialism, their common enemy."[56]

As with all other Soviet attempts to court religious circles, the idea of an alliance between Marxists and liberation theologians, or "rebel priests," was based on deception. Marxists only availed themselves of "progressive" Christians and theologians in order to attain political power. What counted for them was the so-called "balance of forces." Realizing that the Catholic Church in Latin America could not simply be ignored, they pursued a policy of divide and rule by promoting inner strife and conflict, thus turning the church into their battleground.

Liberation theology, therefore, did not serve the cause of political freedom and human rights. It served, in the end, the cause of Marxist rule. The best example of this was the Sandinist rule in Nicaragua, where the Marxists used liberation theologians to legitimize their power. None of these liberation theologians and political priests protested press censorship, practices of torture in Nicaraguan prisons, suppression of the peaceful opposition, and violations of human rights.

Concluding Comments and additional remarks on KGB infiltration of the WCC and the role of Islam

The 1975-1986 period has seen an increasing effort on the part of the Soviet Communist Party and its allies to use religious groups and personalities for political propaganda. These efforts were part of an overall policy of manipulation and deception, prepared and carried out by the International Department of the CPSU through the Russian Orthodox Church and several of its front organizations. A supportive role was played by the KGB (the former Soviet Security and Intelligence Service) which had its own specialists dealing with religious matters. Other special interest groups - such as scientists, physicians, trade unionists, politicians, and even former NATO generals - were targeted as well. One of these former NATO "Generals for Peace" even received money from the East German Secret Service. This is what Werner Grossmann, former East German Secret Service Chief, told me in a TV-interview that I had with him in August 2001. (Grossman, by the way, was the successor of the legendary East German Spy Chief Markus Wolf.)

Whereas Marxists-Leninists rejected any real blending of religion and ideology, they did not oppose "common action" between communists and religious forces. The fact that the radicalized religious elite often did not see any contradiction between religious experience and Marxist convictions made it susceptible to the totalitarian propaganda of the former communist states. I still remember quite well how senior staff members of the Lutheran World Federation (LWF) in Geneva felt attracted to "Maoism" in the 1970s.

There were, in addition, also a great number of religious fellow travelers, who fell for the sweet language of "peace" without realizing that it could very well be employed in the interests of maintaining and even expanding a system of injustice and suppression. As in biblical times, many in the religious world have not learned to discern the false prophets crying, "Peace, peace!" when there is no peace (Jeremiah 6:14). Suppression of human rights and keeping nations in bondage against their will are incompatible with peace. This is what Mikhail Gorbachev, the last Soviet party leader, intended to change.

After the dissolution of the Soviet Union in December 1991, the World Peace Council continued to exist, although without financial help from Moscow. The relatively short Gorbachev era also ended in December 1991. The Christian Peace Conference ceased to exist in 2001.

Vasili Mitrokhin, who supervised the transfer of the First Chief Directorate's archive from the Lubyanka to the new KGB headquarters at Yasenovo, defected to the United Kingdom in 1992. This First Chief Directorate was responsible for the KGB's foreign operations and intelligence activities. Mitrokhin and Christopher Andrew, a leading historian from Cambridge University, published the book *The Mitrokhin Archive* in 1999. Both authors quote from a KGB report saying its agents had succeeded "in placing its agent KUZNETSOV in a high WCC (=World Council of Churches) post." This was at the WCC Central Committee meeting in Canterbury in 1969. "Agent KUZNETSOV was Aleksei Sergeyevich Buyevsky, lay secretary of the Moscow Patriarchate's foreign relations department headed by Nikodim. Throughout the 1970s and 1980s he played an active role in the work of the WCC Central Committee, helping to draft policy statements on international affairs."

I identified the late Aleksei Buyevsky as a possible KGB agent already in 1977 - in my book *Christus of Ideology? (Christ or Ideology?)*, a lengthy study on church-state relations in Nazi Germany, the Soviet Union and Communist China. This was based on personal observations at WCC meetings, not on any other sources. It was a guess at the time and my guess turned out to be correct. Mitrokhin and Andrew further point out that the late metropolitan Nikodim was a KGB agent codenamed ADAMANT.[57]

In the 1970s and 1980s the Soviets had a keen interest in the Muslim world, although there was no Islamic equivalent to the Christian Peace Conference. They supported Palestinian terrorist organizations and initiated an international debate on "anti-Zionism." When Muslim extremists forced the pro-Western Shah of Iran to flee his country and took over in January 1979, the Soviets did not hesitate to court the new rulers.

A setback, though, was the Russian invasion of Afghanistan in December 1979, which was universally condemned by the Muslim world. The Soviets continued, however, to manipulate anti-Semitic public opinion in the Middle East and Iran, often successfully. Their vocal criticism of Israel and Zionism was helpful in this respect. In October 1980, Syria and the Soviet Union signed a twenty-year Treaty of Friendship and Cooperation. During the Iran-Iraq war (1980-1988) the Soviets reiterated that they were neutral, yet they sided with the ruthless Iraqi dictator Saddam Hussein, a secular Muslim, providing him with arms. After that war Moscow's relations with Iran suddenly improved. Iran and Syria are now Russia's most important allies in the Muslim world.

(This book was first published as chapter 9 in the reader *The New Image-Makers. Soviet Propaganda & Disinformation Today* edited by Ladislav Bittman (Boston University), Pergamon-Brassey's International Defense Publishers, Inc., Washington, New York, London, Oxford, Beijing, Frankfurt, São Paulo, Sydney, Tokyo and Toronto (1988). The text of this book has been edited, modified and updated

The new Soviet leader Mikhail Gorbachev received Patriarch Pimen in the Kremlin in Moscow in April 1988. (Journal of the Moscow Patriarchate.)

by me in the Autumn of 2016. Ladislav Bittman was a former Czech (communist) intelligence officer who defected to the West and became director of the study of Disinformation and associate professor of journalism at Boston University. He is also known as Lawrence Martin-Bittman.)

Notes

1. Karl Marx and Friedrich Engels, *On Religion* (Moscow: Progress Publishers, 1975), p. 39.
2. V.I. Lenin, vol. 15 of *Collected Works* (second printing) (Moscow: Progress Publishers, 1973), p. 405.
3. Ibid., p. 408.
4. "Telegram from His Holiness Patriarch Pimen to Premier A.N. Kosygin," *Journal of the Moscow Patriarchate no.* 1 (1973), p. 1.
5. World Council of Churches Central Committee (Toronto), *Minutes and Records* (Geneva: World Council of Churches, 1950), p. 91.
6. David M. Paton, ed., *Breaking Barriers: Nairobi 1975* (London and Geneva: Society for the Promotion of Christian Knowledge (SPCK) and World Council of Churches, 1976), p. 169.
7. Ibid., p. 174.
8. Patriarch Pimen, "Letter to Edward Scott, Moderator WCC Central Committee, and Dr. Philip Potter, General Secretary, WCC," *Journal of the Moscow Patriarchate* no. 4 (1976), p. 14.
9. Based on the author's personal observations at the WCC Assembly in Nairobi, December 1975.

10. Helene Posdeeff, "Die Rolle des Moskauer Patriarchats in Nairobi (The Role of the Moscow Patriarchate in Nairobi)," in Peter Beyerhaus and Ulrich Betz, eds., *Oekumene im Spiegel von Nairobi 1975* (Bad Liebenzell: Verlag der Liebenzeller Mission, 1976), p. 247.
11. "WCC Officers Call for Removal of Soviet Troops from Czechoslovakia," *Ecumenical Press Service* no. 31 (August 1968), pp. 2, 3.
12. "The Rev. Dr. Philip Potter, WCC General Secretary, Visits the Soviet Union," *Journal of the Moscow Patriarchate* no. 8 (1983), pp. 66-67.
13. Author's personal record of the press conference of the World Council of Churches at the Vancouver Assembly, August 18, 1983.
14. For more extensive treatment of this, see J. A. Emerson Vermaat, "The World Council of Churches and the Afghanistan Crisis, 1980-1984," *Conflict Quarterly* (University of New Brunswick, Canada) 5 (1985), pp. 5-18.
15. Ibid., p. 14.
16. Paul Abrecht and Ninan Koshy, eds., *Before It's Too Late: The Challenge of Nuclear Disarmament* (Geneva: World Council of Churches, 1983), p. 3ff.
17. "Speech by His Holiness Patriarch Pimen of Moscow and All Russia, at the Plenary Meeting of the Soviet Peace Committee," *Journal of the Moscow Patriarchate*

no. 5 (May 1984), p. 39; see also *Nederlands Dagblad*, October 19, 1983, p. 2.

18. *Izvestia* (Moscow edition), June 18, 1969, as translated in *Current Digest of the Soviet Press* 21, no. 28 (1969): p. 20.

19. "Communiqué of the Meeting of the Representatives of the World Religions," *Journal of the Moscow Patriarchate* no. 12 (December 1973), p. 31.

20. This is what happened to the author of this book.

21. See the complaints of Russian Orthodox Bishop Feodosiy, in a letter to Leonid Brezhnev, dated October 26, 1977, in *Glaube in der Zweiten Welt* (Zurich) no. 2 (1982). 55ff. On state control over the church, see the "Secret Report by the Deputy Chairman of the Council for Religious Affairs, Mr. V. Furov" in *Glaube in der Zweiten Welt* no 11 (1982), p. 1ff.

22. Leopold Labetz, ed., *Solzhenitsyn: A Documentary Record* (Harmondsworth and Baltimore: Penguin Books, 1974), p. 297.

23. The pro-Soviet line of this conference was obvious from its documents, which were published in *Journal of the Moscow Patriarchate* no. 8 (August 1977), p. 18ff.

24. "Appeal by Heads and Representatives of Churches and Religious Associations in the USSR to the Leaders and Followers of World Religions on Problems of Disarmament and the Consolidation of Peace among Nations," *Journal of the Moscow Patriarchate* no. 8

(August 1981), p. 3.

25. "International Inter-religious Meeting: Report by Metropolitan Filaret of Minsk and Byelorussia," *Journal of the Moscow Patriarchate* no. 12 (December 1981), pp. 33, 45.

26. J. A. Emerson Vermaat, "De Rol van de Russische-Orthodoxe Kerk in het Sovjetrussische Vredesoffensief (The Role of the Russian Orthodox Church in the Soviet Peace Offensive)," *Militaire Spectator* 154 (2), p. 84; Binnenlandse Veiligheidsdienst (BVD), *Een verhulde factor in de kernwapendiscussie* (A Hidden Factor in the Dutch Discussion on Nuclear Weapons in the Campaign Against Nuclear Weapons), pp. 31, 32, an excellent confidential Security Service report, February 15, 1981.

27. J.A. Emerson Vermaat, "The KGB and the West European Peace Movements," *Midstream* 30, no. 5 (1984), p. 10.

28. Rotterdam's and Amsterdam's daily newspaper, *NRC-Handelsblad,* May 12 and May 18, 1982; *Hervormd Nederland (The* Hague), May 22, 1982, pp. 7, 8.

29. Prague's *CPC Information* no. 257 (1979): p. 8ff. See also U.S. Department of State, *Soviet International Fronts* (Washington, D.C.: Government Printing Office, 1983).

30. The documents were published in the *Journal of the*

Moscow Patriarchate no. 11 (1982), p.2ff.

31. N. Kovalski, "Religious Forces Against War Threat," *International Affairs* no. 7 (July 1983), p. 51.

32. See, for example, the press release *News from the USSR,* no. 79 (The Hague: Embassy of the USSR, 1983), pp. 1-8.

33. "Meeting at the Soviet Peace Committee," *Journal of the Moscow Patriarchate* no. 3 (1984), pp. 40, 41. See also Metropolitan Yuvenaliy, "New Public Commission," *XX Century and Peace* no. 2 (1984), pp 15-17.

34. Most of the front organizations are discussed in Clive Rose's *Campaigns Against Western Defence: NATO's Adversaries and Critics* (London: Macmillan, 1985), p. 246ff.

35. World Peace Council, *Program of Action 1981* (Helsinki: Information Center, World Peace Council, 1980).

36. On the CPC, see in particular William C. Fletcher's *Religion and Soviet Foreign Policy 1945-1970* (London: Oxford University Press, 1973), p. 39ff.

37. J. A. Hebly, *Strijd om Vrede: Essays over Kerken in een Marxistische Samenleving (The Struggle for Peace: Churches in a Marxist Society)* (The Hague: Boekencentrum, 1983), pp. 52ff, 62.

38. Nikolai Ryzhkov, "To the Participants in the Seventh General Conference of the Asian Buddhist Conference for Peace," *Buddhists for Peace: Journal of the Asian*

Buddhist Conference for Peace 8, no. 2 (1986): 10. Ryzhkov's message was also published in *Izvestia* (Moscow edition), February 13, 1986, p. 1.

39. On Niilus's appointment, see Eugene Carson Blake's "The World Council of Churches: East-West Church Relations 1966-1972," in Ans J. van der Bent, ed., *Voices of Unity* (Geneva: World Council of Churches, 1981), pp. 8, 9. I saw Niilus at many WCC meetings. He appeared to me a political fanatic.

40. Niilus's presence in Sofia was confirmed to the author at a press conference during the WCC Central Committee meeting in Dresden, the German Democratic Republic, August 1981. Koshy's presence in Prague had been noticed by the author when he covered the WPC's "Peace Assembly" for the Dutch Press.

41. "World Public Opinion and the Second Special Session of the United Nations General Assembly Devoted to Disarmament," *Final Report of the Conference Convened by the Special NGO Committee on Disarmament* (Geneva: World Council of Churches/Commission of the Churches on International Affairs, 1982), p. 4.

42. *Peace Courier* (extra supplementary edition) 15, no. 4 (1984), p. 8.

43. Leo Schellekens, letter to the editor, *De Volkskrant* (Amsterdam's daily newspaper), May 19, 1984, p. 19. Also, the Socialist International is a group of social

democratic parties in Europe.

44. Paulos Mar Gregorios, "Address to the Sixth ABCP General Conference," *Buddhists for Peace: Journal of the Asian Buddhist Conference for Peace* 5, no. 2 (1983), pp. 4-5.

45. *Journal of the Moscow Patriarchate* no. 5 (1983), pp. 35-58.

46. The accounts and documents of these conferences have been published in the following issues of the *Journal of the Moscow Patriarchate:* no. 6 (1984), pp .34-57; no. 5 (1985), pp. 30-53; no. 9 (1986), pp. 37-57.

47. J. A. Emerson Vermaat, "The Unique Experiment: the WCC In Central America," *Freedom at Issue* (Freedom House, New York) no. 91 July-August 1986), p. 19.

48. David E. Mutcher, *The Church as a Political Factor in Latin America* (New York: Praeger Publishers, 1971), p. 124.

49. Gustavo Gutiérrez, *A Theology of Liberation* (London: SCM Press, 1975), pp. 112, 202.

50. Ibid., pp. 233, 272-279.

51. Basic Document Adopted by the International Conference of Communist and Workers' Parties in Moscow of June 17, 1969, in *Pravda,* June 18, 1969, as translated in *The Current Digest of the Soviet Press* 21, no. 28 (1969), p. 20.

52. K. Khachaturov, "Imperialism and the 'Rebellious

Priests' in Latin America," *International Affairs* (Moscow) no. 9 (September 1977), p. 84.

53. Lazar Velikovich, "Latter-Day Inquisitors," *New Times* (Moscow) no. 26 June 1985), p. 22.

54. Ibid., p. 23.

55. Adolf Nika, "Wie Moskau die Theologie der Befreiung Sieht und Beurteilt (How Moscow Views Liberation Theology)," *Materialdienst* 49 (1986), pp. 172-173.

56. Alvaro Oviedo and Stepan Mamontov, "Theology of Liberation: A New Heresy," *World Marxist Review* 29, no. 3 (1986), p. 90.

57. Christopher Andrew and Vasili Mitrokhin, *The Mitrokhin Archive. The KGB and the West* (London: Allen Lane, 1999), p. 636 (Nikodim), p. 637 (Buyevsky); J.A.E. Vermaat, *Christus of Ideology? (Christ or Ideology?)* (Utrecht: De Banier Publishers, 1977), p. 226. "Indien Buyevsky zelf niet tot de geheime dienst behoort, dan staat hij toch zeker onder directe controle van de Russische geheime dienst, alleen al uit hoofde van zijn functie." See also: Emerson Vermaat, *De Evangelische Omroep - Ontstaansgeschiedenis (Founding History of the Evangelical Broadcasting Corporation)* (Soesterberg: Aspekt Publishers 2007), pp. 36, 37, 126 footnotes 35 and 36. "EO" was founded in 1967 and is part of the Dutch public broadcasting system. I worked for them as a news reporter specialized in the ecumenical movement, international affairs, war reporting, terrorism, Latin America and Eastern Europe (July 1973 through December 2004).

that the higher ROC dignitaries, who are allowed to visit the Netherlands or to have contact with Dutchmen at CPC or WPC conferences, belong exclusively to the first two categories, who are listed by name.
There are a number of indications that the KGB, which has a separate directorate operative in the churches, had penetrated deep into the ROC hierarchy and for instance/imposes certain obligations on ROC dignitaries travelling abroad. Moreover the ROC hierarchy openly declared "its support for the peace-loving external and internal policy of the great and beloved fatherland". The head of the ROC, patriarch PIMEN of Moscow, stated on 7 May 1980 on radio Moscow that "we must aim at stopping the armaments race in Europe and North America, a race which has become particularly dangerous as a result of the NATO decision to station new American nuclear missiles in Western Europe". This is the line of agreement followed by ROC representatives when presenting the case for peace and security abroad.

For some time there has been an increasing number of visits to the Netherlands by ROC dignitaries, although the Dutch ROC province probably does not number more than about a thousand members. From the meagre information available it appears that the visitors are usually interested in CPC activities or contacts with peace organisations and denominational parties. From 3 - 12 October 1989, for instance, there was a ROC delegation here, which gave the purpose of its visit as "consultations with Dutch religious denominations", but which was really intent on establishing contacts with political parties and peace movements. All these meetings were arranged by the third secretary Political Affairs of the Soviet Embassy, I.A. KROTOV, who is suspected of having KGB affiliations. Another striking fact is that the metropolitan of Minsk and white Russia FILARET had, since he became Exarch for Western Europe in December 1978, paid at least five visits to the Netherlands for reasons not known. What he came to the Netherlands to do could be deduced from the fact that in 1979 he was awarded two decorations for work for peace in the

A page from a lengthy and confidential Dutch intelligence ("BVD") report on Soviet attempts to manipulate the peace movement (February 1981). There is a Dutch and a shorter English version of this report.

Box MPM/1981

VS-VERTRAULICH
amtlich geheimgehalten

Linksextremistische Einflußnahme auf die "Friedensdemonstration" am 10. Oktober 1981 in Bonn

Inhalt		Seite
1.	Veranstalter der Demonstration	1 - 2
2.	Entstehung des Demonstrationsaufrufs	3
3.	Unterstützung durch Linksextremisten	4
3.1	Orthodoxe Kommunisten	4 - 8
3.2	"Neue Linke"	8 - 9
4.	Reaktionen der Linksextremisten	9 - 11
5.	Beurteilung	11 - 12

Anlage: 1) "graswurzelrevolution" Nr. 9/81

2) aus: "Kommunistische Volkszeitung" Nr. 42 vom 16.10.1981 (Seite 3)

Two pages from a secret German intelligence report on Soviet attempts to manipulate the peace movement in Germany (October 1981).

Linksextremistische Einflußnahme auf die "Friedensdemonstration" am 10. Oktober 1981 in Bonn

1. Veranstalter der Demonstration

Die beiden offiziellen Veranstalter der Demonstration am 10. Oktober 1981 in Bonn, die "Aktion Sühnezeichen/ Friedensdienste e.V." (ASF) und die "Aktionsgemeinschaft Dienst für den Frieden" (AGDF), sind keine extremistischen Organisationen. Sie haben jedoch Verbindungen zu orthodox-kommunistischen Kreisen; vor allem zwischen ASF und Kommunisten besteht seit Jahren eine Zusammenarbeit.

So waren AGDF und ASF bereits auf dem von prosowjetischen "Weltfriedensrat" (WFR) initiierten "Weltkongreß der Friedenskräfte" im Oktober 1973 in Moskau vertreten. Ein Delegierter der ASF nahm auch an dem vom WFR veranstalteten "Weltparlament der Völker für den Frieden" im September 1980 in Sofia teil. Auf diesem Treffen forderte Boris PONOMARJOW, Kandidat des Politbüros und Leiter der Internationalen Abteilung des ZK der KPdSU, den "Friedenskampf auf ein neues Niveau zu heben". Dazu sei eine "weitestgehende Aktivierung der politischen und gesellschaftlichen Kräfte" erforderlich (Zit. nach "Beiträge zur Konfliktforschung", 2/1981, S. 130 ff.).

Die ASF gehörte dem orthodox-kommunistisch gesteuerten "Westberliner Vorbereitungskomitee für die X. Weltfestspiele der Jugend und Studenten 1973" in Berlin (Ost) an. Seit 1974 veranstaltet sie jährlich "Festivals der Friedensdienste", an denen sich auch Funktionäre und Mitglieder DKP-beeinflußter Organisationen beteiligen. An zahlreichen Veranstaltungen einer "Friedenswoche" unter dem Motto "Frieden schaffen ohne Waffen", zu der die ASF erstmals für den 16. bis 22. November 1980 aufgerufen hatte, nahmen auch orthodoxe Kommunisten

Ministerium für Staatssicherheit
Hauptabteilung XX
Leiter

BStU
000076

Berlin, August 1988
XX/4/IV/kB-ar

16413

Bezirksverwaltung
für Staatssicherheit
Abteilung XX
Leiter

Rostock

MfS/Ro 16
Eing. 15.08.88
Tgb. Nr. 645
Weiter an:

Koordinierungsberatung zum Interkirchlichen Friedensrat (IKV) der Niederlande

Am 07. September 1988 findet um 10.00 Uhr in der Hauptabteilung XX/4 die nächste turnusmäßige Koordinierungsberatung zur weiteren operativen Bearbeitung des IKV statt.

Es ist vorgesehen, eine Lageeinschätzung seit der letzten Beratung am 14. 06. 1988 vorzunehmen und die operativen Aufgabenstellungen abzustimmen.

Sie werden gebeten, einen verantwortlichen Mitarbeiter Ihrer Diensteinheit mit der Teilnahme an der Beratung zu beauftragen.

i. V. Paroch
Oberst

Secret report from the East German Secret Service ("MfS") on attempts to infiltrate the Interchurch Peace Council (IKV) in the Netherlands – "Koordinierungsberatung zur weiteren operativen Bearbeitung des IKV," August 1988. These attempts were not successful. The MfS was more successful in financing the "generals for peace movement" whose chairman was Michiel von Meyenfeldt. Von Meyenfeld was also chairman of the IKV between 1975 and 1977 and he was on the IKV's speakerslist and advised the general synod of the Reformed Churches in the Netherlands. But IKV general-secretary Meint-Jan Faber did not like von Meyenfeldt's courtship with the communists in Eastern Europe in the 1980s. See Emerson Vermaat, 2Vandaag TV, 22 August 2001, http://zoeken.beeldengeluid.nl/internet/index.aspx?chapterid=1164&filterid=974&contentid=7&searchID=1944425&columnorderid=-1&orderby=1&itemsOnPage=10&defsortcol=12&defsortby=2&pvname=personen&pis=expressies;selecties&startrow=1&resultitemid=3&nrofresults=5&verityID=/14140/17349/17290/54842/81264@selecties.